LANDSCA
QUILTING FOR
BEGINNERS

The Picture Step by Step
Guide on How to Make
Landscape Quilts at Home
Including Landscape Quilt
Patterns and Designs

Boris Joseph
Copyright@2022

TABLE OF CONTENT

CHAPTER 1
INTRODUCTION

Are you able to see them?!
Nature has imprinted all of those
lovely leaf patterns on the
bedsheets herself! Yes, those
impressions of leaves were
created by 'Mother Nature'
herself through the process of
Eco Printing; there was no
drawing or painting involved in
the process. Who knew
bedsheets could be so
aesthetically pleasing?!

This Art Quilt with a basic design may be hung on a wall or used to keep you warm. Believe me when I say that it isn't that tough (this is also my slogan, by the way).

Greys and beige colors are incredibly relaxing and flexible in today's world of technology. There's nothing better than these neutral prints, and the pattern is rather flexible to deal with as well. Use my design or come up with your own landscape; it's not as time-consuming as the conventional, brightly colored ones that granny used to create (that we feel guilty about not using or liking).

CHAPTER 2
STEP BY STEP TO MAKE LANDSCAPE QUILT

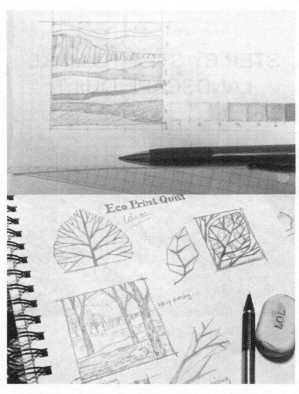

Every excellent thing begins with a well-thought-out strategy. If you know me or have visited my website, you will notice that my designs have a rustic feel to them and that I get much of my inspiration from nature. The beauty of a forest never ceases to astound me, and this is true in all seasons of the year. 'How beautiful it is to watch the shadows dance across the hill...

As you walk backwards through a scene, the tones and colors grow more grey. This is the inspiration for the landscape design. The foreground becomes darker and then appears to be getting closer.

Create a grayscale of the general tones to see where they will work best in the environment. If you squint your eyes, you will notice less detail, but the overall 'value' of the grey will be more apparent to you. That is how designers conceptualize their designs. I utilize the grey scale to match each cloth to its appropriate location in the design.

This design seemed to be the perfect fit for my growing collection of "carrier blankets" and eco prints, which I had gathered as a result of my extensive "Eco printing." There was not a single fabric pattern purchased!

Download the pattern from the link below:

Attachments

file.name is being downloaded.

Quilt - madebybarb.pdf is a PDF document.

Download

Step 2: This is where the magic takes place:

Don't you simply stand there in awe when you notice the intricate features of leaves? Each species possesses a unique set of characteristics, including varied amounts of tannins and the ability to produce stunning prints. Yes, the reds are magnificent, but they do not print in that manner! It's a long road of tests, but when the magic comes, it's absolutely amazing.

The Fabric consists of a variety of fibers that are woven together to form a fabric.

The fabric I chose for these is 100 percent cotton since 'Mother nature' does not like to print on non-natural fibers, which is why I used cotton for them. Used bed sheets are an excellent source of fabric. It is essential to thoroughly scour your cloth to ensure that there is no residue left on the fibers. Use approximately 1 tablespoon of washing soda to 1 gallon of water, as well as around 2 tablespoons of detergent to complete the cycle (do not use fabric softener). Use the hottest water you can get, or even better, boil it for a couple of hours to get the best results. Don't be startled by the large amount of 'yellow water' that comes out!

The Leaves are a type of plant that grows on trees.

Certain types of leaves have favorable effects. My personal favorites include maples, sumac, rose leaves, and eucalyptus (a particular kind), but there are many, many more species out there that differ from nation to country. You may use them right away or dry them for later use. India Flint has some excellent recommendations as well.

The Mordant (pronounced "mordant"):

In order for the color dyes (reactions of tannins with mordant) from the leaves to cling to the fiber permanently, a mordant must be used to produce a 'bite' in the fiber. Iron* will have the effect of a mordant. The preparation of an iron water solution is as simple as assembling a collection of rusted iron artifacts, water (such as railroad spikes), and vinegar. It may be necessary to do certain experiments in order to determine the strength of the iron. Soy milk is another pre-mordant that should be avoided. Soak overnight, then rinse well before using. Taking many dips will also be beneficial.

The necessary supplies are as follows:

To wrap the strips of cloth around, large dowels or pipes are utilized, which are then connected together with rope to make a tight roll.

* When working with solutions, use caution and wear gloves.

3rd Step: How Does the Magic Work?

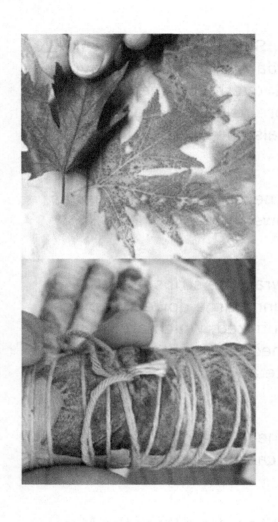

16

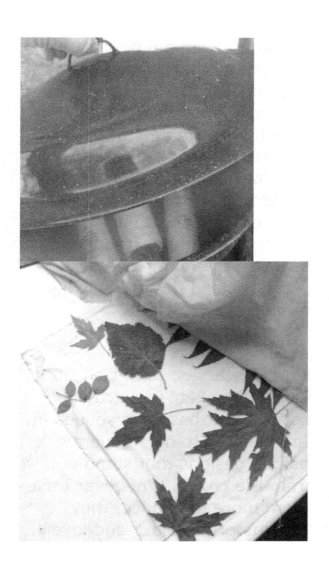

The iron water can be incorporated into the fabric by dipping it or by soaking the leaves in it for a short period of time (approximately 30 minutes). The leaves are put on the cloth, which is then firmly coiled up in a tube. A barrier layer of plastic wrap or parchment can be wrapped in between the fabric layers to prevent bleed through between the layers.

For my scarves, I print on silk with a "blanket" (a piece of cotton) that has been soaked in "iron water" to help generate unique designs that stand out from the crowd. Whenever I use them more than once, they become pretty black and lovely.

There are just a few alternatives for processing, including steaming, boiling, and digging into compost piles (pew, I have not tried that one). It might take anywhere between 1 and 2 hours to see results.

But when it's time to unroll (as soon as it's cold, or let it sit for a longer period of time if you have the patience), it's like Christmas morning. Because tiny changes in fabric, mordant, iron strength, plant species, and other factors can all have an impact, it is impossible to predict exactly what you will receive.

They are cleaned and washed when the printing process is completed. They can even go through the laundry, however certain detergents include harsh ingredients such as enzymes, making it necessary to use a softer PH neutral soap instead.

Step 4: Easy-to-use Tools and a Template

20

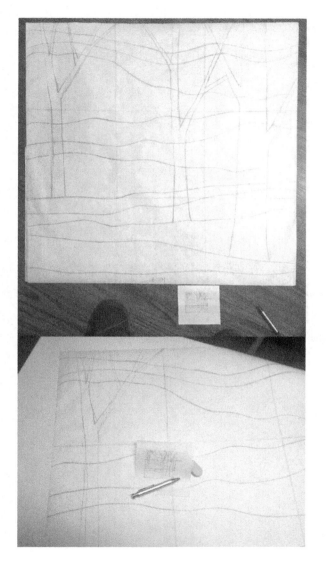

21

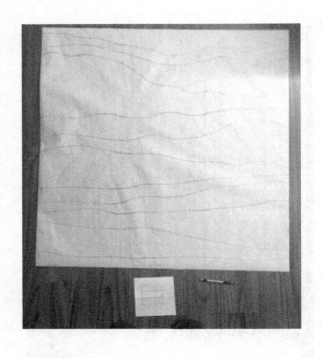

When it comes to traditional
quilts, they may be a pain to put

together. They are quite time-consuming because to the repeating nature of the design. This one is more 'rustic,' thus there is no way that the design can go horribly wrong.

The following are the essential items required for the sewing project:

Eco-printed cloth with a pop of color for the border (yes, all were once a bedsheet)

excellent shears

rotary cutter (sometimes spelled rotary cutter) (makes it so much easier) a mat for cutting (to save your table)

pattern

Sewing machine is a machine that sews things together (basic straight stitch type will do)

a strand of yarn (obviously, matching colours and also some invisible thread)

pencil

a measuring tape

Quilt Batting is a type of fabric that is used to make quilts (polyester or cotton fibre)

Following the creation of the pattern, you will be required to create a big full-size replica of it.

When scaling up a picture, it is important to employ a grid system as a guide. Make the equal number of squares on both sizes, and then work your way up from tiny to giant, square by square, starting with the smallest size (basic artist method). They're just wavy lines in any case, which is one of the reasons I adore this style; it's so simple. Approximately 36" by 36", my primary picture square.

I produced two versions of the design, one with trees and one without.

The Fifth Step is to Cut the Curves.

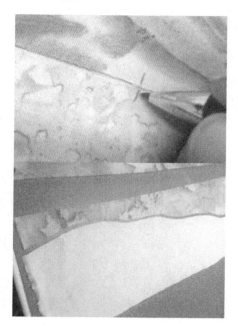

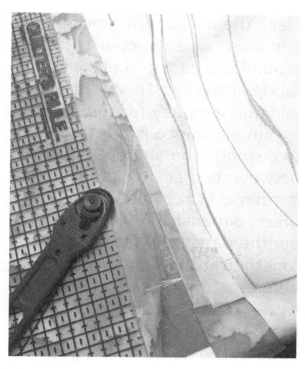

At first, I was a little intimidated by the prospect of sewing curves, but it turns out to be rather straightforward! Who would have thought it?

Place the design on the cloth and allow an additional 1/4 inch around the edges "a piece of fabric at the top This will be the additional money for the quarter "seam allowance is a term used to describe the amount of space between two seams in a garment. (Take note of the green dimension.) If required, pin the paper and fabric together at the first curve line before cutting through them with a rotary cutter. You may use two layers to cut the next edge at the same time if you want to. Alternatively, you may just run the cutter down the edge with additional fabric piled behind it.

Work your way around the curve one curve at a time. I put the paper back together with a couple pieces of tape to keep everything together.

Make a few little lines to make sure that the curves are of the same length.

Curves are sewn in at the end of Step 6.

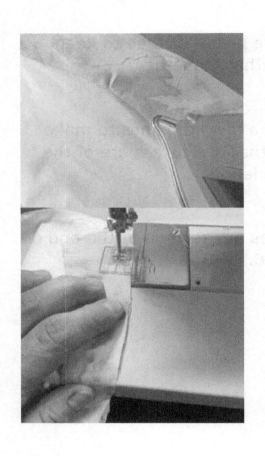

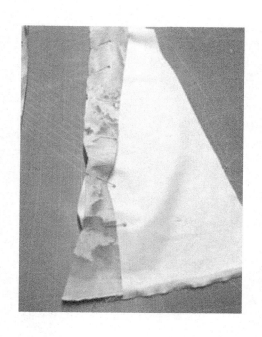

Place the curved fabrics next to one other and make sure the edges are aligned. Pins can be used, as well as marks that must be followed. It is a quarter "seam and will allow you to stitch the edges together more easily as you go.

As you stitch, make sure that the fabric is smooth and that no little creases appear. Slight pushing on the curves helps to flatten them.

Seams should be pressed to one side.

The seventh step is to sew all of the other curves.

The ease with which you can stitch a curve will become apparent once you have completed a few. Continue using the same concept for the rest of the group.

Keep in mind to factor in an additional 1/4 inch "seam allowance as indicated at the top of the design.

Using the extra 1/4 yard of fabric, trace the design onto the cloth "a piece of fabric at the top (working top to bottom)

Cut a curve through the paper and cloth you're working with.

Remove any excess fabric and insert the next fabric beneath the curve edge to create a replica.

matching the edges and sewing them together (right sides facing)

to one edge, steam press thoroughly

— repeat the process with the following curve.

8th Step: The Section titled "Tree Line":

A distant tree line is depicted in the design, which is made up of strips that are joined together to make a single curve. They are shaped like triangles in order to resemble trees. Choose a few hues that are in the middle of the spectrum (not too dark or too bright). It is usually beneficial to examine patterns from a distance in order to determine their total worth.

Cut a few triangle strips at random and alternate the designs. It is important that they be longer than necessary since they will be cut later (which is MUCH simpler than fiddly perfect pieces!)

Check the fit of the design on your body.

Step 9: Sew the Tree Line Strip to the top of the tree:

44

Assemble the parts by sewing them together in alternate directions in the triangular shape. Because of this, the strip will be quite straight and will include a few tree-like forms. Seams should be neatly pressed.

To trim the curve shape, simply follow the steps outlined previously.

Continue with the next bends all the way to the bottom. Each time, compare the tones to one another to see how they compare.

Using free motion sewing, sew the trees together in a circle.

Was it less difficult than you anticipated? Beautiful scenery in this shot! Whether it's on a beach or in the desert, we want trees.

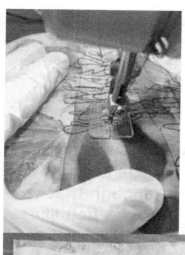

I've been having a lot of fun with free-motion stitching, so I decided to make some 'crazy trees'!

Make sure the presser foot is applying only a little amount of pressure (loose enough that you can slide the fabric as you like). It was not necessary for me to alter the foot (there are some available)

There is also a suggestion to use embroidery hoops as an alternative. Yes, if it is something you would like to do. Rubber gloves were worn to ensure that I maintained strong grip on the fabric while stitching, which ensured that the fabric remained flat during the process.

The cloth is not rotated; rather,
it is simply slid in whatever
direction that you like by the

50

user. Yes, it appears to be a bit of a mess, but it IS a tree!

To make the trees, I used the darkest eco prints I had saved for this project. The most prominent foreground tree should be the darkest, with the remaining trees becoming lighter as they progress into the distance. (Yes, I do paint from time to time...)

Cut strips that taper as they rise and are long enough to fold under approximately 1/4 inch on each side "less than or equal to

Plan the pieces on the pattern before cutting them out. Fold the edges under and iron them well.

Transfer the trees to the cloth and secure them with pins. Keep an eye out for overlapping. The closest tree should overlap the ones at the back, and so on.

Step 12: Putting the Trees Together:

Originally, I had planned to do some painting in the trees. That is also possible, but you would have to begin earlier in order to complete all of the curves. (Perhaps the next one)

Top stitching is a simple and effective method of attaching the trees. Using matching thread or invisible quilting thread, sew as near to the edge as you can without the thread slipping off.

Keep an eye out for a layered transition from the background trees to the foreground, and lift branches to sew back the ones that need it the most.

The nice thing about them is that you can make them as wavy or as straight as you like. There are no rules when it comes to trees! Perfect!

Step 13: Trimming the Accent Bands at the Bottom and Top:

As part of my effort to create a tall quilt, I included several "design features." I really like all of the nuances that the eco prints create, so I wanted to show off a few more of them.

I prefer to be free of precise forms, so I cut a number of strips of varying widths and prints from a range of sources.

My mum used to do some strip-quilting in her spare time. Essentially, the idea is to sew strips together lengthwise first, and then cut them into strips to help the process go more quickly. That makes putting the pieces together a LOT less time-consuming. (This was one of the reasons I didn't want to make quilts.)

Attaching the Accent Bands is the fourteenth step.

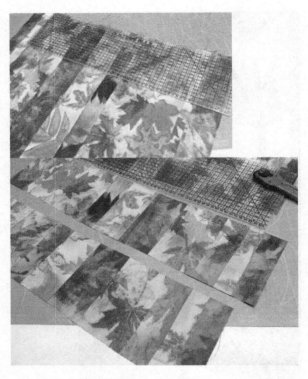

Once the strips have been sewed and pressed together, split them into strips and, if necessary, piece them back together.

The primary picture and the accent are both surrounded by a small white border (2.5" - 3.5") in the original drawing. This maintains it looking new and well-defined. (Again, the bed linens)

Sew the white border to the bottom and top of the main design (using the press), and then sew on the accent strips to finish it out.

Wow, things are moving along very rapidly here...

Step 15: Increase the size of the borders:

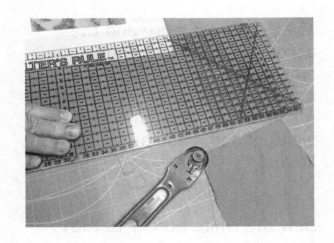

The bigger medium grey border (which is made from another bed sheet) is ideal for hiding dirty finger prints... You may make it as broad as you like.

To make borders, I prefer to tear long pieces since it assures that the border is precisely straight. Easy-peasy.

Sew and press in a nice and orderly manner. It's a thrill to be so close to finishing...

Step 16: Injecting a Little Softness Into the Mix:

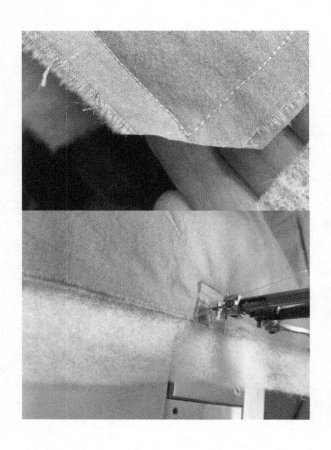

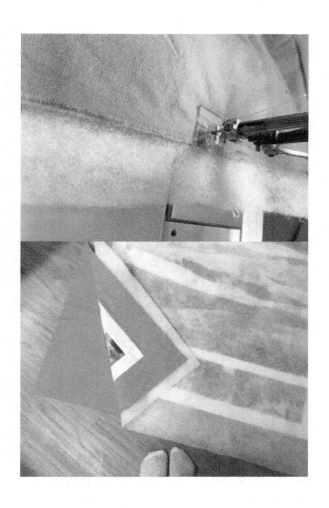

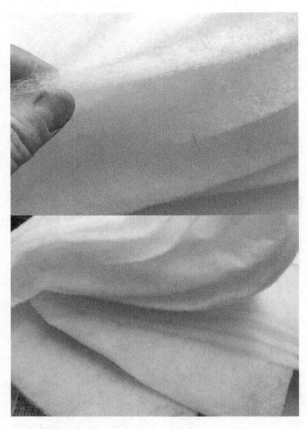

Quilt batting comes in a variety
of colors and textures to help
keep quilts warm. You may
choose between incredibly thick
and thin fabrics, cotton or
polyester, or even silk. Storage,

washing, and stitching through the quilt are all things that come to mind.

I choose for a thin batt that is nonetheless pretty warm despite its thinness.

Measure and cut a rear panel that is the same size as the front panel. If necessary, put it back together.

Lay down the entire quilt on a big flat surface (like the floor), with the back and front panels facing each other and the binding in the center. Either put the batt on the floor or on the top and secure it with a lot of pins.

Sew all the way around, leaving a little hole for turning (like making a pillow). Sew with the fabric side facing up to avoid getting the batting trapped in the foot of the machine.

Once you've finished sewing, turn the stitches at the corner and cut the corner.

Turning the quilt is the seventeenth step.

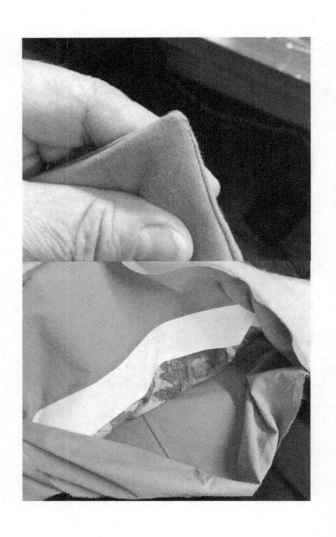

It is referred to as 'birthing' the quilt in the quilting community since it is the process of turning the quilt inside out of the enormous rectangle pocket.

In order to obtain nice points, use the blunt end of anything to press the corners outward.

Pin the opening closed to make it easier to hand stitch it closed.

Run stitches that alternate between the top and bottom of the garment and are properly hidden are recommended. This completes the quilt's main body.

'Stitch in the Ditch' is the 18th step.

After the 'birthing,' it's time to get to stitching.

Pin all of the layers together tightly, making sure that everything is completely flat.

The advantage of invisible thread is that you don't have to worry about finding a matching color. It's also quite nice. Take a look at the difference between the visible and invisible samples.

Because I am a hurried individual, all of the finishing is done by machine. Alternatively, you might hand-stitch all of the quilting. The'stitch-in-the-ditch' technique worked really well for this pattern. The stitching is used to retain the batting in place on the interior of the quilt.

I snip the threads once I've finished stitching everything to save time. Roll the sides of the quilt to reduce the amount of bulk you have to move to get to the center. Pant clips were formerly a staple in my mother's wardrobe. Due to the fact that this is a little quilt, it was simple and quick to complete.

Step 19: You will adore, adore, adore your cozy, warm quilt:

Move over, stodgy old-fashioned
quilts, and make way for the hip
and trendy 'Art quilt'! Excellent
use of grey and neutral tones.

Not to add that there were no fabric designs purchased (they were really affordable) and that just bed sheets were used. Check the linen closet for a moment...

The one-of-a-kind prints are quite intriguing to look at since there is so much detail in each cell of the leaves.

It's very magical! I really appreciate how the prints are haphazard and surprising. In our current high-tech environment, we simply like bringing in the 'warmth' of nature, particularly rough and tactile materials such as live edge wood. These rustic designs are just excellent for adding a touch of character.

So practical for keeping you warm and snug... it's as though Mother Nature is wrapping her arms around you!

If this is something you are interested in, you may also purchase a silk scarf or manufacture one yourself.

Step twenty-one:

THE END

Made in United States
Orlando, FL
27 November 2024

54512369R00049